The Future of Religion

The Future of Religion

Interviews
with Christians on the Brink

Bob Harvey

Foreword by
Michael W. Higgins

NOVALIS

© 2001 Novalis, Saint Paul University, Ottawa, Canada

Cover: Blair Turner

Layout: Gilles Lépine and Francyne Petitclerc

Business Office:
Novalis
49 Front Street East, 2nd Floor
Toronto, Ontario, Canada

M5E 1B3

Phone: 1-800-387-7164 or (416) 363-3303
Fax: 1-800-204-4140 or (416) 363-9409
E-mail: novalis@interlog.com

Canadian Cataloguing in Publication Data

Harvey, Bob

The future of religion: interviews with Christians on the brink

ISBN 2-89507-109-8

1. Christianity–20th century. 2. Christianity–Forecasting.
3. Christians–Interviews. I. Title.

BR100.H37 2001   270.8'2   C00-901698-8

Printed in Canada.

We acknowledge the financial support of the Government of Canada through the Book Publishing Industry Development Program (BPIDP) for our publishing activities.

NOVALIS

Contents

Foreword 7

Introduction 10

Donald Akenson
History Professor, Queen's University 15

Karen Armstrong
Bestselling Author 27

Harvey Cox
Professor, Harvard Divinity School 41

Douglas Hall
Retired Theology Professor,
McGill University 51

Janine Langan
Culture and Christianity Professor,
University of St. Michael's College 61

Victoria Matthews
Anglican Bishop 71

Ernie Regehr
Peace Activist 84

Ron Sider
Co-founder of Evangelicals
for Social Action 95

John Stackhouse
Former President of the Canadian
Evangelical Theological Association 105

Will Sweet
Philosopher 117

Foreword

I am not inclined to neologisms. In fact, I find them rather irritating, in the manner of professional jargon-makers. But I do think that with this volume by Bob Harvey, Religion Editor of the *Ottawa Citizen*, the occasion to create a new word is before us.

What you have in this volume is a series of "miniviews." The miniview is a hybrid or combination of the traditional profile and the standard interview. It is a condensation of them both with the added bonus of a touch of reportage. Harvey is rather good at the genre.

As you read further in this volume you will discover an eclectic, rich and colourful constellation of religious figures shaped into attractive cameos. Harvey clearly takes seriously the job of communicating in popular and accessible language the often complex and handsomely variegated world of genuine religious thinking. And so we have a generous smattering of Anglicans, Baptists, Roman Catholics, and Evangelicals, with a Mennonite, a United Church divine and, to avoid the criticism that we are denominationally defined, a freelance monotheist.

All the subjects of Harvey's miniviews are interesting folk. That is not arguable. They run the gamut in terms of background, personal biases, aesthetic and spiritual, confessional links, disciplinary prejudices, age and gender. In fact, they are fully representative of that wild spectrum that we call Christian opinion. You will find between these covers church personnel, seminary instructors, historians, writers and activists. Harvey allows them to think; his probes are honest and unnuanced. In short, what you see is what you get. And that is a relief.

Editor Harvey has a good ear for the jarring phrase, the insightful blurb, *le mot juste,* and the provocative utterance. Writer and historian Don Akenson reminds us: "I personally have a terrific amount of faith and almost no belief"; British savant Karen Armstrong opines: "It's better to see religion as an art form, which elicits within us a sense of transcendent wonder and awe and meaning.... It's like when you listen to the last quartets of Beethoven; it's very difficult to say what this means, or define the conviction you have when you listen to it that life has some ultimate meaning after all"; and then there's the *enfant terrible* of 1960s thinking, Harvey Cox: "We're moving into a stage, in Christianity especially, but also in some other religious movements, in which the strictly cognitive element is of diminishing importance."

All of the subjects in this slim volume are thinking and feeling religious people. They may define theology differently than most in institutional structures, or they find themselves at odds with contemporary trends and movements, but they are all genuine searchers, men and women resolved to explore in a serious and not glib way the implications of religious belief in a time of accelerating crisis.

Bob Harvey's miniviews whet the appetite for deeper probing. And that is as it should be. The reporter has done his job.

Michael W. Higgins

Michael W. Higgins is President of St. Jerome's University, Waterloo, Ontario, and the author of several books, including *Heretic Blood: The Spiritual Geography of Thomas Merton* and *The Muted Voice: Religion and the Media.*

Introduction

This book had its beginnings as an *Ottawa Citizen* project intended to mark the 2000th year since the birth of Christ. The editor of the *Citizen*, Neil Reynolds, called me into his office and suggested I interview a selection of Christian thinkers of my choice. It was a dream assignment: *carte blanche* to pick topics reflective of current Christian thought, meet the thinkers on their home ground, and take up as much space as I needed in the daily newspaper. Over a period of about two months, I visited London, England; Boston; Philadelphia; and seven Canadian cities from Vancouver to Antigonish, Nova Scotia.

The assignment was typical of Neil: imaginative, intellectual and reflective of his conviction that readers are actually interested in religion. The boom in religious book publishing over the last decade should be ample evidence for anyone on that subject, but Canadian newspaper editors are still skeptical that religion is news. Neil is among the growing few willing to put religion on the front page instead of burying it in the ghetto of a Saturday religion page.

What I will most remember about the interviews included in this book is their intimacy. For a few hours with each person, I probed and questioned as we engaged in a dance of the minds. As we talked, I saw new ways of looking at the challenges of technology, or the end of Christendom, or the influence of the Bible on Canadian history. There were even a few rare and wonderful moments when, together, we discovered some new thought or perspective. In those moments, I experienced what I think British writer Karen Armstrong meant when she described her way into God's presence: through a moment of intellectual insight so surprising and so obviously right that it can only have come from some transcendent Other.

Five of my interview subjects were people I had at least met in ten years as the *Ottawa Citizen*'s religion editor. The other five were people I had always wanted to meet. All were thinkers whose work I admired.

My subjects included Victoria Matthews, an Anglican bishop; Ron Sider, a Canadian-American evangelical whose compassion for the poor has launched a new social justice movement in the U.S.; Will Sweet, a Catholic philosopher; Ernie Regehr, a Mennonite and anti-nuclear lobbyist; and Harvey Cox, the Harvard academic, who electrified me way back in the 1960s with his proclamation that it was time to shake off all the rules of the old church, and bring in a new way of doing church.

All of the thinkers I interviewed are heroes of a sort, for they have one of the most difficult callings of any Christian: to go alone into their studies, and struggle to find new solutions to the trends all of us see, but too few of us understand. Their issues are some of the most troubling of our time, including feminism, secularism, the decline of manners, the nature of God, and nuclear war.

Together, they represent a unique cross-section of Christian thinking in our time and, for the most part, in our unique Canadian context. Although the importance of national boundaries is fading, we still need the peculiarly Canadian insights on God and the constitution contributed by Vancouver's John Stackhouse, or Douglas Hall's reflections on living next to the American Empire.

I would also argue that Canada not only needs its Christian thinkers more than ever, but that we are now edging into a new era where their contributions are being heard in a new way. It is clear to all of us now that Christians are in a minority, and that we have precious little political power. For that reason, the contributions of the wider Canadian church's bishops, intellectuals, writers, and pastors are more insightful simply because they stand apart from both power and the latest fashions. Their only real power base now is the counter-cultural insights of the Gospels themselves.

I hope you enjoy meeting these ten men and women as much as I did.

Bob Harvey

Rod MacIvor, *Ottawa Citizen*

Donald Akenson

History Professor, Queen's University

D on Akenson is in awe of the Bible. "As a cultural product, it makes Walt Disney look like an idiot. It covers everything – the big problems of birth and death and why we're here. It's wonderful," says the Queen's University history professor and author of *Surpassing Wonder: The Invention of the Bible and the Talmuds.*

Akenson's acclaimed book argues that the Bible is the central shaping force of Western culture. Never mind the Greeks, he says. It was the Jews who shaped Western civilization.

As he and I sit in the office-loft of his 1871 farmhouse, about 30 minutes' drive from Kingston, Ontario, a westerly autumn wind is whistling and banging at the big windows around us. He perches on his office chair, wisps of hair peeking out from under his black baseball cap, gazing past his computer across more than a mile of open fields.

His relationship with the Bible seems schizophrenic. As a historian, what he can see and research is the work of human hands, and that's the level on which he writes. His personal beliefs are another matter, as private and perhaps as difficult to explain as yours and mine.

What's the greatest idea of all time? I ask him. "Simply that I am not the centre of the universe. Until I realize that, I cannot act as a moral person," he says. "You can learn that idea from any number of religions, or you can learn it from science. That is the single idea around which all civil society revolves."

That idea is certainly central to the Bible. What are some of the other biblical ideas that have shaped our way of thinking?

He tosses off a couple of important concepts: the notion of social contract holding society together, and a belief underlying the entire Bible and our concept of history – that time has a beginning and an end, instead of being cyclical, as the Hindus view it.

But then he chuckles and turns irreverent, even shockingly funny.

Although he is an Anglican and shows every sign of being in awe of the creative force behind the Bible, he also has an outrageous, impish sense of humour. It is part of what makes him original and a delight to read.

"The great ideas in the Bible are: Yahweh's a prick. He's just impossible," Akenson says. "He's totally unpredictable (in the earlier parts of the Old Testament). He's unjust about half the time. That's not bad, in a sense, because that's the way actual life is. The rain falls on the just and the unjust. Secondly, the only way to deal with something of greater force than you – this is what the Bible really teaches – is to kiss its ass. That's all Yahweh really wants. He's a classic Middle or Near Eastern aristocrat, which is to say, he has to be propitiated. And he in fact confirms the rightness of his being in power by being totally arbitrary, being terrifying."

Twenty years ago, when the Bible was new to me, and I took it more literally, I might have been offended by Akenson's remarks (as many people will no doubt be). But his comments are so unexpected on what is normally a "sacred" subject that I can't help but laugh, and I will laugh time and again in the two hours we spend together.

"One of the things you watch happening in the later scriptures and then in Christianity is theologians trying to come to the conclusion that God is good," he says. "Well, God may be good, but there is no way you can infer that from either the Christian or Jewish scriptures." To take some of the edge off his words, he adds: "I am really incredibly respectful of these texts, but I'm not a bishop and you're not one of the clergy."

But he continues: the Bible also teaches that if people are not like us in religion, race or colour, we're not to have anything to do with them. "We're to be hateful, bigoted, xenophobic, homophobic, the whole thing. That's what the children of Israel were taught to be, that's what Paul teaches us to be. Even soft Christian theology teaches that 'if you do not believe what we do, you're eternally damned.' That's a fairly big one. That's the content of the book, and it works. Behind the nicey-nicey we all get from every Reform rabbi, and every Christian who tells us to love each other, we at the same time have these basic things that are at the very core of our animal nature, that we affirm and we detest. We get it both ways."

Akenson says the writers of the Bible were clearly human, and the man who started it all by putting together the first nine books, Genesis to Kings, was not only the world's first historian, but its greatest religious genius ever. "The only question is: Did God direct man?"

In his book *Surpassing Wonder,* he makes a point of writing that the book is "belief-neutral." Readers can see the Bible as the work of God or the work of human genius, as they choose.

So I ask: Do you think there is any role for God in the Bible and in history itself?

"The answer to your question 'What about God?' depends entirely on the assumption you start with," he says. "If you start with the assumption that I'm a historian talking to you as a historian, there's nothing happening that in any way is different than explaining how the Bell phone book came into being. The Bible is just a much better phone book." A clergyman, however, would say that God drives the universe, and therefore, God is responsible for the phone book.

"I personally have a terrific amount of faith and almost no belief," he says. "But in a weird way I do have faith in a universe that, though it looks cold, is benevolent – and though it looks chaotic, I don't think the order we see is just a subset of chaos. But that's my emotion, my assumption or my experience. It's not in any way a rational explanation of the thing I'm talking about."

I want a clearer answer, so I press him: "Are you saying that in some sense you have faith in God?"

"You could call it that. I don't mind. Once I'm not wearing the historian's hat, I could affirm everything in the prayer book. I read a couple of prayers in the morning," he says, nodding to a 1928 Anglican prayer book on his desk. He picked it up in New Zealand for 50 cents.

"If I'm just being a human being, someone who's got kids, been sick, seen a fair amount of people die, I have no trouble going into a totally different set of explanations. The most important things in life are probably non-verbal. If somebody's sick, don't tell them God did it. Just hold their hand."

Weeks later, I telephone him and try one more time to sort out whether he thinks God somehow had a hand in the Bible.

"I'm a Christian, and I believe in some way God directs history," he says. It's a clear, direct answer, but I feel like I've pushed him into an answer he didn't want to give. It's so glib, it does not sound like him.

Akenson is an outsider to biblical scholarship, yet with enough of a scholarly reputation, and enough Hebrew and Greek, to make it difficult for even full-time biblical scholars to criticize him as a know-nothing.

He is one of the world's leading experts on Irish history, and a prolific writer: the author of seventeen non-fiction books and five novels.

Surpassing Wonder was a candidate for the Governor General's Award for English non-fiction and was chosen by the Los Angeles *Times* as one of the best non-fiction books of 1998.

His latest biblical book – *St. Saul: The Skeleton Key to the Historical Jesus* – was published in 2000.

He predicts that *St. Saul* will cause more controversy than *Surpassing Wonder* has, because Saul's letters are generally believed to be the earliest Christian writings we have, and they say relatively little about Jesus the man.

Today, Akenson says the Bible helps hold nations, groups and sometimes even families together. It's what he calls an example of primary literature, one of the few culture-shaping books that people created long ago to mediate between themselves and the terrors of the world.

"They are the ones that deal with the absolutely fundamental questions: What is the nature of the universe? How did the universe get there? Why aren't we doing well? How can we do better? Who are our enemies? The fact is if you're going to pay attention to anything, you're going to pay attention to the primary literature, and the Bible is one of them. There are four or five others in the world. The primary literatures are, in their nature and in their depth, absolutely different than anything else; even the highest art isn't in the same game. Why it is that primary literatures were developed so long ago, rather than recently, is an interesting question. Maybe when they developed they made the development of further primary literature unnecessary."

By definition, primary literature is religious, because ultimate problems are religious problems. Among others on his list of primary literature are the Koran, the Ulster cycle in Irish literature, Homer's *Iliad* and *Odyssey*, and the *Epic of Gilgamesh*, the Sumerian tale of a hero who flourished around 2500 BC.

* * *

What is central to his understanding of the Bible, and its effect on Canada and other parts of the world, is that it is constantly being "reinvented."

In *Surpassing Wonder,* he writes that "A truly great invention ... keeps on developing long after its inventors have declared it complete." The comment is meant to apply to the Talmud (the body of Jewish law that grew from the Old Testament), but he says it applies to Christian and Jewish scriptures alike.

Akenson says every people, every denomination, stitches together its own Bible by selecting bits and pieces from the Bible or other available primary literature, such as the Koran, and mixing it with their own traditions. "Each distinguishable culture gets to make its own Bible, and that's why the Bible works for each of these cultures: they have been able to pick and choose and make from the basic elements a machine that absolutely fits what their culture needs."

South Africa's Boers, Northern Ireland's Protestants, and Israel's ultra-orthodox Jews, for example, all focused on the Old Testament and its emphasis on the right of a chosen people to hold the land given to them by God. Americans have historically emphasized a similar notion, what they called "manifest destiny": God's backing for their expansion into territories such as Texas, California, Alaska, Hawaii and Guam.

According to Akenson, the Bible of Roman Catholics includes papal encyclicals, Catholic canon law, and Christian tradition. The primary literature of the Jews includes not only the Old Testament, but also the Mishnah (legal traditions), and the Babylonian and Jerusalem Talmuds, or commentaries. In each group, "the Bible is only one part of the scriptures. Each tradition develops in addition to those strictly written scriptures a continuous set of traditions that themselves become 'scriptures' as they're written," he says.

Protestant groups also have their tailor-made but often unwritten sets of scriptures. The classic example, he says, is the Southern Baptist convention, the largest Protestant group in the United States.

"It's a set of belief tests that make the Anglicans' 39 articles of faith look really simple: You've got to be suitably homophobic. You've got to be anti-abortion, plus you have to be able to go through a set of rituals that are just as tough as those of the Hasidic Jews, except they don't admit you have to go through it. You have to be able to adopt certain postures, you have to learn the secret vocabulary, you have to learn how they accent certain syllables of certain words. You know, there are certain code words, like 'witness,' and you say 'Jeeesus.' "

He adds, "Protestantism has developed its own bigger scriptures, too, except it has refused to admit it. This is always the trick. The more you do something new, the more you deny this."

I have read *Surpassing Wonder,* so I know the answer to my next question. But I ask it anyway. "Is that a pattern in the Bible itself?"

"Sure, that's where you learn it. The whole Bible. The simple one is the New Testament. It is a total rejection and cannibalization of the Jewish scriptures, total conversion of whatever serious meaning you can get out of the Hebrew scriptures, but yet it takes it and turns it 90 degrees. It works a treat. But that's what the rabbis do with the Hebrew scriptures [in the Talmud]. They take out the parts of Leviticus they're not very keen on. Watch the rabbis explain away anything they don't like."

But what about Canadians? What Bible shaped our culture? "We didn't have to buy into Native American myth or go into the Roman pantheon [of gods]. We had something that was already in some of the best, most compelling English, absolutely compatible with the culture we wanted."

The primary literature that shaped Quebec's historic Catholic culture is relatively easy to understand. "Until 1970, to pick an arbitrary date, Quebec was one of the two classic cases in the world of ultra-montane Catholicism [favouring absolute papal supremacy over national or diocesan authority]. What we call the theocracy was able to sell an entire belief system, of which the Bible was only one segment," he says.

This fervent Catholicism allowed Quebec's bishops to wield immense influence in politics, education, the social services and the family, but also to send far more than their share of missionaries around the world.

In English Canada, the influence of the Bible was more subtle, he says. Like other democracies, Canada is based on a notion of social contract that first originated in the contract between God and his people Israel. Many of the pioneers who opened the Canadian West also shared the American notion of claiming a land promised by God. Later, Tommy Douglas and other preachers of the social gospel helped found the Co-operative Commonwealth Federation (CCF), and its successor, the New Democratic Party.

Akenson is a transplanted American, a Minnesota Swedish Baptist who grew up memorizing the King James Bible, and came to Queen's University in 1970 after teaching at Harvard and Yale.

He has researched nineteenth-century parliamentary debates in Canada and the U.S., and says Canadian politicians have never practised the rolling religious rhetoric of the Americans. "There is this wonderful Canadian sense of cool. The temperature of everything in Canada has almost always been lower than elsewhere. It's kind of self-bonding to quote the scriptures. 'Here's my view, and by the way God agrees.' In part, that's civil manners. How do you explain it? One of the things I love about Canada is that there has always been such a subtle culture. It's all done in shades of grey. There is no technicolour. Just to learn those discriminations and watch that is glorious. You can have high art, at this little end of the spectrum."

Karen Armstrong

Bestselling Author

God is with us always, say the world's major faiths. But who is God? The warlike God of the early Jews? The personal, rational God of today's Western Christians? Or, perhaps, some other God that we have yet to discover?

Karen Armstrong's answer, in her best-selling book *The History of God*, is that we have created many different gods, and they are now an endangered species.

In the concluding chapter of that book, she writes: "How will the idea of God survive in the years to come? For 4000 years it has constantly adapted to meet the demands of the present, but in our own century, more and more people have found that it no longer works for them, and when religious ideas cease to be effective, they fade away. Maybe God really is an idea of the past."

If God is a mere idea, then I want to know who it was that Jesus and the Jewish prophets claimed to know. And if there is to be a future God, who might it be? So I visit Armstrong at her home, a gentrified Victorian row house in north London.

She is a former nun, and was for seven years in the 1960s a member of the Society of the Holy Child Jesus. She was sent to Oxford to prepare for a teaching job with the order, then stayed on at Oxford to complete a doctorate, permanently leaving the order.

Years later, epilepsy forced her to quit teaching at the University of London, and she wrote a scathing autobiographical critique of religious orders. That, along with her wit and her provocative opinions made her the darling of Britain's media, an all-purpose expert on everything religious.

Since then, she has poured out book after book, including a biography of Mohammed, and *Jerusalem*, a religious history of the city. This year alone, she's finishing up three more books: a biography of Buddha, a history of Islam, and a massive tome, *The Battle for God*, on the rise of fundamentalism in Christianity, Islam and Judaism.

When she began writing, her first agent told her that religious books would never sell. He is no longer her agent.

She says her books sell because "people are thirsty ... to find something that doesn't just cling to one parochial vision of one single denominational truth. Instead of seeing your own quest as a sort of lonely, idiosyncratic thing, you see it's part of the universal quest for meaning, a human thing, and we've kept on in all the traditions coming back to the same solutions, and the same kinds of ideas, and for many people this is affirming."

One of the reasons she left the convent was her own struggle with God. "I used to hate God," she says. "He was always grousing away about how I hadn't said my prayers properly, jotting down on some giant computer all my errors and mistakes. He'd be up there waiting for me when I died. I hated this. He was never satisfied."

* * *

Now she sees her own early notion of God as limited and eccentric, and for a while she called herself an atheist, after rejecting that God. But during the five years she spent researching and writing *The History of God*, she found a much richer view of God in all the great world faiths. Now she quotes freely from Jesus, Mohammed, Buddha, and Islam's Sufi mystics, and styles herself as a "freelance monotheist."

Armstrong, slim, short, blondish, and just short of her 55th birthday, greets me at her door. As we talk, it is difficult not to notice the engaging gap between her front teeth; it gives her an eager urchin look that takes some of the edge off her intensity and her sharp criticisms of Western Christianity and its leaders. Yet she talks faster – at least 130 words per minute – and more provocatively than anyone I have interviewed.

Voltaire said that if God did not exist, we would have to invent him. I ask her why we need a God.

"We don't necessarily need a God or a supernatural personality, a sort of cosmic big brother ... but we are creatures that need meaning in our lives ... and if we can't build a faith into our lives we seem to fall into despair," she says. "In all the major world faiths, a similar faith has evolved; it is remarkably similar across the board, a transcendence that is both within and without each human being."

I pause and search my memory for a definition. What is transcendence, anyway? Something beyond the limits of ordinary knowledge and experience. Yet I and many others know we have touched something or somebody in moments of meditation, or even during a walk in the woods. So I ask: What is this presence we feel, if not God?

She gives a long answer: "We can never say what it is, because it is transcendent. If we think we've got God and can define God, this is just a creation of our own. It's very often a creation of God in our own image and likeness. That has been one of the pitfalls of monotheism, particularly in the Western world, that we've thought it possible to define what God is."

She continues, "I had to learn a definition of God in the Roman Catholic catechism, at the age of eight. This is a mistake. The most advanced and thoughtful monotheists in all three traditions (Christianity, Judaism and Islam) have insisted that what we call God bears no relation to the ultimate reality. In fact, they've gone so far as to say it's better and more accurate to say that God does not exist because our notion of existence is far too limited to apply to the divine, the sacred. They've said that God is Nothing with a capital N ... that God is nothing because God is not another being, not something tacked on, not an unseen reality like the atom that we can discern by means of logical enterprise."

If we can't truly describe God or know God, then what is the point of worship services and all the doctrines of organized religion?

"It's better to see religion more as an art form, which elicits within us a sense of transcendent wonder and awe and meaning," says Armstrong. She gestures to her sound system and a large rack of CDs. "It's like when you listen to the last quartets of Beethoven; it's very difficult to say what this means, or define the conviction you have when you listen to it that life has some ultimate meaning after all. That's what religion should do for us, and that's what doctrines should do for us: not define things, but hold us in a state of wonder and awe."

I can relate to religious experience as artistic experience, but I insist that, in rare moments, there's an experience that goes beyond just art. Something unearthly seems to show up, I say.

Yes, she says. "But probably not 'something.' A thing is another reality. But a certain transcendence is a fact of human life. It has been an absolute fact of human life. We have always sensed this transcendence, and we have created and found it always in symbols down here below. We have experienced it in something else, in scripture, in a mountain, a sacred place, a law code, or a human being, man or woman. That has been a common experience of sacredness, but once you start saying exactly what it is, then you are cutting it down to size, your own size."

Is there anything, anyone really there?

"We don't know. All we know is what we have experienced. Buddha was very sensible about this. When asked 'Does Nirvana exist?' or 'Does a Buddha, when he's achieved enlightenment, exist in Nirvana?' he said these are entirely inappropriate questions because we have no words to describe this.

"Buddha says if you live in a certain way, practise compassion to all beings, if you meditate and get in the habit of getting in touch with these deeper currents of consciousness, if you always try to speak accurately ... then Buddha says you will know, you will have intimations of what Nirvana is, but you will never be able to define it, because it is something else."

Does she ever experience this transcendence?

"I can't talk to God. I can't do it. I can't meditate, either. I was such a flop at meditation in the convent. I was so bad at it – it was a form of meditation that didn't suit me, and I am filled with utter exhaustion at the thought of doing it. But I do get moments of complete awe and wonder and transcendence, upstairs in my study. Just seconds of it. That's what Jews say they have in studying Torah. St. Benedict made his monks engage in what he called *lectio divina* (reading followed by reflection) and in the midst of it he said they would have mini-seconds of *oratio*, or prayer. I think that is a form of spirituality I stumbled on unawares."

* * *

Armstrong says that each person has a different conception of the divine, because no one concept is adequate. What's more, each of us experiences the divine differently.

"The rabbis in the Talmud said that when God appeared to Moses on Mount Sinai, every single one of the Israelites who stood at the foot of the mountain had an entirely different experience of the divine, because of their personalities. It's another way of saying that the little old Italian lady and the sophisticated theologian will have different notions of God, but each one is valid."

In *The Battle for God*, released in March 2000, she explores not only fundamentalism, but also the birth of modern consciousness in the sixteenth century. She says part of that modern consciousness is a literal reading of scripture, and Western Christianity has gone badly wrong since it became too rationalistic.

"I think the embattled nature of a great deal of 20th-century discourse, not just the fundamentalists, but the more orthodox people, is defensive because they feel they are sitting on some volcano. That if these things aren't facts, then the whole thing isn't true. Well, that would have seemed inconceivable to a pre-modern person."

In pre-modern religion, there were two ways of apprehending reality, she says. "One was called *mythos*, one was called *logos*. *Mythos* was intuitive, meditative ... part of the mind; mythology was never intended to be taken literally. Nobody would have been stupid enough to imagine we could prove how the Exodus from Egypt happened – or who split a sea in half to create a new reality, or how people went into the deep and came out the other side as an important rite of passage. So to try to account for the historical reality of the Exodus by pointing to the frequency of flash-flooding in the region is to totally miss the point. But in the West, starting in the sixteenth century, *logos*, science, began to achieve such spectacular results that *mythos* became discredited. In order to make religion respectable, people started to translate the myths, the *mythos* of their religion into *logos*, and to say these were facts. We started to read our Scriptures in a literal way, which is entirely new, a modern way."

She adds, "We've got stuck in the West in a rut of literal reading of Scripture, and many people, let's face

34

it, never have the chance, nor are they helped by their clergy, to develop beyond an infantile notion of God. We're told about God the Father when we're kids in Sunday school, and we're told these stories of the flood. While we've revised our notion of Father Christmas or Santa Claus, and seen that it's a myth, we don't very often do that revisionist process with God, and we retain these infantile notions of the divine until we're old people."

What would happen to church attendance in the West if the mythological nature of religion was taught once again?

"I think things might perk up a bit. But it's not just that you've got to teach it in your head. You've got to *do* it, too. Remember what the Buddha said: You've got to live in a certain way. People don't realize this is a whole way of life. It comes also with cult and ritual and also practice – compassionate, ethical practice. Recognizing sacredness in other human beings is part of the deal. If people saw the churches concentrating more on compassion and not endlessly haranguing them about their beliefs and their sexual behaviour, I think they would come back to church. Charity and compassion are seen in all the major world faiths as the litmus test for any true theology; that's crucial to the New Testament. As St. Paul says, you can have faith that moves mountains, but if you lack charity, it's worth nothing. That was the message of Jesus again and again, but we've lost touch with that. The idea of compassion is that it makes you unseat the ego, yourself, from the centre of the universe, and put another person in there instead."

Then what is it we are to seek in life? God or compassion?

"Seek ultimate meaning. And you do it by living as fully as you can on all levels. The tried and tested way of doing that is by these rituals of compassionate living, accuracy of speech, not lying, and learning to wake up to the full potential you have."

I remind her that at the end of *The History of God*, she has suggested that the time for an idea of God is past.

Her clarification surprises me. "No, what I say is the idea of religion will always be with us. I always say that if God, the old God, works for you, the old idea of the personalized deity, even the old man with the white beard, works for you, then stick with it. If it makes you compassionate, that's the test Jesus gave. If it makes you self-righteous, belligerent, unkind, chauvinistic to others, then it's probably not a very good idea of God."

I toss out one of my stock questions: "What was the greatest idea of all time?" And, as always, it shows that even hard-nosed critics of religion see hope somewhere.

She tells me that what is of supreme importance is "not so much an idea, but a conviction that we can make ultimate sense of our lives. We're not imprisoned in our suffering, or hopelessness, or misery, but we can ultimately transcend it with a great deal of hard work."

What about predictions for the religious future? She says that in the immediate future, fundamentalism will be with us in all the major faiths. As Western modernity spreads, fundamentalist movements spring up beside it everywhere. Pluralism, a new appreciation of other faiths, is also going to be with us, she says. It's already changing the way many people experience faith. They're turning to other religious traditions for spiritual nourishment. More Christians than Jews read Jewish philosopher Martin Buber. Jews study Buddhism and read Christians such as Harvey Cox and Paul Tillich. Jesuit priests go off to learn meditation from Zen monks. We are realizing that other faiths have something to say to us.

I finally come to the question to which Ms. Armstrong has devoted a whole chapter in *The History of God* – an issue that she says may be the topic of her next big book: What will our future notion of God look like?

"My belief is that we are just too hung up on things like the ideas about God. We should get back to getting rid of the idea of God and, exploring that a bit more, being aware that our symbols are only symbols. We should live in the way the Buddha says: Don't ask inappropriate questions that can't be answered, and don't expect instant answers, instant conceptions of God, instant theologies. These will evolve in the case of one's religious practice. Religious practice helps to build up an attitude which helps us to have religious experience."

But, at the end of our long conversation, she admits that this idea of the future of God may be mistaken, too. She says each of her books began with an idea that was discarded within the first three months. Ultimately, she struggles through to fresh insight, and the new book emerges four or five years later.

Her idea of God is still evolving, too.

Harvey Cox

Professor, Harvard Divinity School

In 1965, a 34-year-old Baptist minister prophesied the collapse of traditional religion.

Harvey Cox wrote that "secularization simply bypasses and undercuts religion and goes on to other things. The age of the secular city ... is an age of 'no religion at all.' It no longer looks to religious rules and rituals for its morality or its meanings."

For me and many others who read his book *The Secular City* in the 1960s, it was a song of liberation from "dead" religious rules, and a celebration of the freedom to be found in anonymous cities.

The Secular City became an unlikely bestseller of nearly a million copies, and turned its author into one of the English-speaking world's best-known commentators on religion in everyday life. Cox went on to become a professor at Harvard University, and travelled the world, chanting with Hare Krishna, chewing peyote with Mexico's Huicholes, and blending critical analysis with personal reaction in an outpouring of books and articles.

Cox, however, has at least partially changed his mind. In recent articles, he has proclaimed that "secularization is dead," and "the world may be even less secular at the end of the 20th century than it was at the beginning."

I wanted to know more, so I travelled to the Boston area to meet with him. What will happen to religion in the next millennium? I wondered. And how can traditional religion and secularization both be dead? I hoped he would offer some answers.

* * *

As we begin our chat in his Harvard Divinity School office, a nearby tower clock chimes the quarter hour. I'm late, and flustered, having lost my way on the venerable university's sprawling campus, with its mix of historic and ultra-modern buildings. He forgives me with a ready smile. At 70, his rosy complexion and trim figure are aided, no doubt, by the daily four-storey climb to his book-lined office, overlooking one of the school's many green spaces.

On his wall, there's a poster-sized photo of a seventeen-year-old Harvey Cox, shown on his identity card as a merchant seaman on relief ships to Poland and Germany at the end of the Second World War. It is a clue to the roots of his passion for social justice, which would later propel him to work with churches in

Communist East Germany and get him arrested at civil rights demonstrations in the American South.

I begin by asking him why he says secularization is dead.

"I would say secularization is dead as the controlling metaphor, or the most helpful paradigm, for understanding what is going on in the 20th–21st century. There are still processes of secularization going on, and there are also processes of re-sacralization going on, and there is always a contretemps going on between the two, back and forth. When one goes too far, the other kicks in and vice versa. To that extent, you have to say that secularization, in the sense in which I was using it in 1965, as the myth of the 20th century, is certainly not going to be helpful anymore. It might as well be dead," he says with a chuckle.

What does he mean by secularization? One dictionary defines it as the exclusion of religion from the public sphere, in such institutions as schools and legislatures. He says secularization may also mean exclusion of religion from the culturally formative institutions of society, such as television, film and literature.

So where is the evidence that religion is no longer being excluded from such spheres?

He reels off a long line of examples, including Britain's prime minister, Tony Blair, publicly identifying himself as a Christian socialist; Al Gore and George W. Bush Jr., the leading U.S. presidential candidates in the 2000 election, saying government should strengthen faith communities because they're needed to help deal with the nation's social problems; Indonesia electing an Islamic theologian as president; and a renaissance of religious operas in Salzburg, Austria.

All over the world, there is also evidence of a resurgence in religious impulse, if not traditional religious institutions. Cox cites new religious movements in Japan, China's Falun Gong meditation movement, and the million young people who flocked to see John Paul II at World Youth Day in Paris in August 1998.

"This is really not secularization," he says. "Whatever it is, it's not your normal nineteenth-century expression of religion, either. It's very fascinating but it's hard to see what it is."

His best guess is that European, and perhaps Canadian, traditional religiosity is mutating. He describes it as the internalization or the de-institutionalization or even the decontrolling of religion.

In a recent article in the *Harvard Divinity Bulletin,* he said his tentative conclusion is that "what we are witnessing is neither secularization nor its opposite (re-sacralization). Rather it is a fascinating transformation of religion, a creative series of self-adaptations by religions to the new conditions created by the modernity some of them helped to spawn."

Among other things, this means that he was more right than wrong when he wrote *The Secular City.* He wrote, correctly, that traditional religion was losing its grip, and criticized the traditional churches for not reaching the poor and marginalized, who are now being swept up by Pentecostalism and other new religious movements. He also said that despite the fears of many religious people, God is present in the secular, in those spheres of life that are not usually thought of as religious. That's probably even more obvious today than it was in the 1960s. And secularization is still anything but entirely dead.

Cox says that in some Arabian countries and in parts of India, those who are reacting against draconian forms of traditional religious suppression are radically secular. "Their only answer is to get rid of the whole thing."

Elsewhere, like in the United States or in parts of the Muslim world, fundamentalism is a reaction to secularism, or its close relative, modernity. For some, Pentecostalism, with its emphasis on religious experience, emotionalism and lively music, is an antidote to the dry rationalism of an increasingly technological world.

"In Europe, Pentecostalism is growing most rapidly among the technological elite," says Cox. "These people sit all day looking at these dull screens, and [Pentecostalism] gives them the chance to let it all out. Everybody is emotional at some level. They either get a chance to vent it cheering on the Red Sox, or they go to church. We're moving into a stage, in Christianity especially, but also in some other religious movements, in which the strictly cognitive element is of diminishing importance. There is more emphasis on the symbolic, the metaphorical, the narrative, the liturgical aspect, which is why I really think Anglicans and Roman Catholics and Lutherans and others who have preserved more symbolic eucharistic forms of worship may begin experiencing a lot of return of people who are looking for this sort of thing. Oddly enough, Pentecostals are more like that than they are to the middle of the road," he says.

Although secularism and what we now call modernity were essentially born in the United States, the whole world often seems to be increasingly Americanized. I ask: Are there countries more American, more secular, more modern than the Americans?

Cox laughs and says yes. "If you travel a lot, the upper élites, especially among young people in Asian countries, are more American than we are. They have really bought the whole thing, lock, stock and barrel. Rock music, the clothing, the language and the world view. The market culture is there. In the U.S. one sees indications of our young people stepping back."

The picture is confusing. What he is portraying is an ocean of opposing currents: fundamentalism and secularization and new forms of religion sweeping across the world, sometimes mixing, sometimes colliding, sometimes throwing off some entirely new form of quasi-spiritual movement.

And the traditional major world faiths are being changed by travel and immigration. Islam is just beginning to be influenced by Muslims who have grown up in the West, while Western Christians are being forced to develop something other than an aggressive evangelism as an approach to the Buddhists, Hindus and Sikhs who now live among them, instead of "over there."

* * *

What, I ask, is the next millennium of religion going to look like?

Cox says we are moving not into a Christian century, as some predicted at the beginning of the 20th century, nor a secular century, but what he calls a "pluriform" one, where we will continue to look to religion for meaning, but will develop many new forms of it.

"It's a world in which we will live with contending and overlapping meaning narratives, some of them explicitly religious, some of them not so religious. And this will require people to take a lot more personal responsibility for assembling what I think of as a collage, putting together a system of practices and beliefs and values that make sense. They won't be simply assemblages that are completely various. They will be obvious extensions of major religious traditions with some things added, some things subtracted. That's what we'll see going on, in part because of the pluriform nature of the cultural and religious environment."

Does he have hope? Yes, because for him, the greatest idea ever is that God is present in human history, suffering, hoping and struggling along with us.

"That's what makes me a Christian. The meaning of the incarnation of Jesus and the Gospel is that we're not alone in the universe, and we have reason to hope. Martin Luther King's big point, which he used to make frequently, is that the universe is on the side of love and integration and justice. We have cosmic allies."

Harvey Cox is the author of several books, including *The Secular City* (1965*); Religion in the Secular City* (1984); *The Silencing of Leonardo Boff: Liberation Theology and the Future of World Christianity* (1988); *Many Mansions: A Christian's Encounter with Other Faiths* (1988); and *Fire from Heaven: The Rise of Pentecostalism and the Reshaping of Religion in the Twenty-First Century* (1995).

Douglas Hall

Retired Theology Professor, McGill University

D ouglas Hall believes it is a good thing that the Christian church, as we have known it in the West, is coming to an end.

For centuries, the church cast its lot with the powerful and warped the Christian message, he contends. "It was ChristenDOM," he says with emphasis. "It tried to be the dominion of the Christian religion. I'm happier to talk about the dominion of Christ, because that is the dominion of suffering servanthood."

The retired McGill University professor of theology is one of Canada's best-known theologians, and a prolific author on many subjects, including the future of the church. His works are clear and forceful.

"The church has to change or die. The only question is: Will it take charge of this change? If it doesn't, it will eventually disappear," he says.

"Whatever is to come would have to be a broader, more inclusive, more humanitarian and creation-centred philosophy."

We met at his home in Montreal, a few blocks from busy, polyglot Sherbrooke Street, and discussed the church, the future and the American Empire over tea at his fine old dining-room table.

In his book *The Future of the Church* he writes: "Biblical faith is not interested primarily in predicting the future, but influencing it." Hall, a United Church minister, may shy away from predicting the future, but he knows what he wants for the future of the Canadian church. He has little use for triumphalist Christianity, the brand that counts success in numbers and conversions.

"Every word of the New Testament was written in the consciousness of the church being in a pluralistic situation, and as a minority, not a majority. I don't think Jesus in his wildest dreams would have thought of the Holy Roman Empire or the United States as Christian countries. All the metaphors he uses are metaphors of littleness: salt to help preserve the food, yeast to make the dough rise."

Minorities can accomplish things that majorities can't, says Hall, including vigilance for the victims that majorities always create. He believes the church must be creative, prophetic and critical. "It can make bedfellows with various causes, but it can't permanently tie itself up with national, international or imperial or racial or economic causes."

He says the dis-establishment of the Christian church, its gradual separation from the political and economic establishment, started at least two centuries ago as Europeans began to find alternatives to the church. But even now, when the people in the pews on a Sunday morning are a minority in Canada, many denominational leaders are shutting their eyes. They believe that "if they just wait long enough, the people will come back, or at least they'll be able to get their pension at the end. It's very repressive. I've been in one church in Montreal that will seat 2000, but if they have 60 on a Sunday morning, including paid choir members, they are very lucky. How dead do you have to get before you realize you're mortally ill?"

If churches must either disappear or take charge of this change, what should they do? I ask.

Hall says what's needed first is a change of attitude, an understanding that things must change. That may mean ministers working part-time in the church and full-time elsewhere. It may mean shedding the burden of huge, empty buildings. It must also involve more theological education for all those Christians who stick around.

"In the future, theologians will be an absolute necessity, because Christendom is no longer with us, and people are not going to fall obediently into the pews. The only thing that will keep the whole thing going is some kind of commitment to ideas. Automatic Christianity is really at an end, and if people do stay around, then it's increasingly because they sense that there's something in this that grasps the whole of them, not just some kind of need for community, but their minds as well."

He believes the great theological task of the future church will be to find an answer to the curses of the 20th and 21st centuries: anxiety, lack of meaning and despair.

He studied at New York's Union Theological Seminary under Paul Tillich, one of the great Protestant theologians of the century. Mr. Tillich taught that Christianity came from a classical culture fixated on faith and death, while the medieval age was fixated on guilt and condemnation. The church found answers to the problems of faith and death in salvation theology, and to the problem of guilt in Christ as the victim sacrificed for humanity's sins.

"The reason that we haven't come to terms with meaninglessness and despair," he says, "is because it is the most difficult of all the anxieties." To understand and solve the problems of meaninglessness and despair, future theologians will personally have to enter deeply into that anxiety, and that carries risks.

"The life of Tillich himself is an indication of how difficult it is, because his life – and others' – was in many ways broken by it," he says.

One of the common North American responses to meaninglessness and despair is what he calls religious simplism. "Because of the complexity and depth of this malaise, anyone with a clear, strong, one-sided message can get an audience. That is the secret of so much American evangelicalism. They're smart guys, smart institutions, because they know perfectly well that people are flailing about. So anyone who says 'This is the way and, indeed, the only way,' will get an audience."

Hall says even intellectuals want the certitude that comes with ideology, which he considers simply a more sophisticated cousin of religious simplism. Doubt is at the base of all theology, he says. "In fact, I can't think of faith in any authentic way without thinking of it as a dialogue-partner of doubt. Paul is always making this thing between faith and sight, in passages like 'Now we see through a glass darkly, then we shall see face to face.' Kierkegaard says faith sees best in the dark. When this faith gets turned into absolutes and certitudes and slogans – Jesus is God and that kind of stuff – it's ideology."

That "Jesus is God" phrase reminds me of the condemnation suffered by the Rev. Bill Phipps, the moderator of Hall's own United Church, after he told the Citizen's editorial board that Jesus is not God.

"I felt sorry for old Bill, he replies." He says if he had been criticized as Mr. Phipps was, he would have reminded his accusers that Christianity decided in the fourth century that it is heretical to say Jesus is God. By saying Jesus is God, you deny monotheism and deny the humanity of Jesus.

Jesus praised God, and those who ignore that "do bad things, not only at the doctrinal level, but also at the ethical level, and at the level of relations with other faiths," he says.

What is the problem at the ethical level? I ask.

If you ignore the distinction between God and Jesus, then you present Jesus as a model of integrity, a kind of perfection of divinity, he says.

We need a more authentic, a more down-to-earth model of Jesus, he says. When he was young, he was told Jesus was exactly six feet tall, and since it was already obvious to Hall that he would never be tall, he found it hard to identify. Women, too, have a problem identifying with a Jesus who is portrayed as a perfect male.

What the church of the future needs is not this idealized Jesus, but the real Jesus, the human one presented in the scriptures as struggling toward unity with God, someone who has to learn obedience through suffering and struggle, he says.

What role will the Canadian church of the future have to play in relation to the American Empire next door? I ask.

"The Canadian situation is unique. We are the only people who live bang up against the empire. And it affects every aspect of our lives. I like what British economist Susan Strange said: Probably the world needs a schoolyard bully, somebody who can show strength against the worst bullies. Of course empire is problematic. But we should try to make it a better empire.

"Americans are by nature believers, and we [Canadians] are skeptics. I think there's something climatological. Northern peoples of the world are not believers. It is also compounded by history. We live alongside an enormous empire, which is more powerful than any empire, and we envy it and fear it. There is some relation between our proximity to power and our capacity for prophetic analysis. I think of John Kenneth Galbraith, the economist, and George Grant, and all kinds of Canadians. George Grant's book *Technology and Empire*, and indeed all of his writings, should be required reading for theological students," says Hall.

I took courses from Geoge Grant at McMaster University, and I tell Douglas Hall of a corridor conversation from the mid-1960s: Grant told me that my increasingly non-Christian generation would remain civilized because of our upbringing in a Christian culture, but our non-Christian children would be barbarians, because they had lost that influence.

It was a remark I shall never forget.

"That's another side of Christendom," says Hall. "It wasn't all bad. I sometimes say facetiously that if all it produced was Johann Sebastian Bach, it was worth the effort. But it produced a whole lot more than just Bach. It produced a whole civilization, a whole culture of art, of literature. Shakespeare is not understandable apart from it. The end of Christendom is not something to cheer about. We have to broaden our vision beyond the narrowly Christian, to become more pluralistic, if we want to preserve what's best in our tradition."

Democracy, in some ways, is also a product of Christianity, says Hall. If we take seriously Calvin's doctrine of the sovereignty of God, it puts kings and presidents, and even concepts, in their place.

When we're answerable to something or someone bigger, he says, it keeps politics and other human concerns in perspective.

"The things we do elevate – sex and pleasure and buying things, acquisition – these are truly pathetic. Little sex was never intended to be God, and it suffers greatly when it's divinized."

No adequate substitute for Christianity is emerging to provide our society with new philosophical underpinnings, he says. As Christendom is dismantled, we are losing many things. We have some responsibility to see that something goes in place that is able in the pluralistic system to maintain some of the things Christianity stood for.'"

One example he gives is marriage. He believes the Catholic bishops in Quebec have some responsibility to ensure that civil marriages become more than just perfunctory events.

"Marriage needs some kind of ritual, the sense of entering something larger than just a covenant between two individuals, if it's going to get through all the slush that goes into the lives of two people trying to live together."

Hall says that for a time, the West may have to go through a mini Dark Age, and the barbarianism beneath the surface of our civilization may even emerge. But eventually alternatives to Christianity will emerge. "We are programmed to prefer life against death," he says.

The only future Christianity he would be interested in would operate in the public arena, would desire to change the world, and would work in partnership with other people and faiths that have a common life commitment.

"Christianity should not lose faith in the real apostolic tradition, but part of regaining that confidence has to be letting go of confidence in power, and getting more confident in the inherent wisdom of the tradition," he says. "I'm not one of those who says Christianity should retire into the wings. We have a tradition full of light, beauty and truth."

Janine Langan

Culture and Christianity
Professor, University of
St. Michael's College

J anine Langan, a University of Toronto culture and
Christianity professor, says the bad manners and
vulgarity in today's society reflect a lack of gratitude for
Creation.

Her criticisms of contemporary culture are deep
and cutting: our manners are declining, our vulgarity
is growing and our relationships are shallow and
fleeting.

"Culturally, we are in a downward spiral," she says
with an accent that reflects her native Paris. Langan
says the evidence is there for all to see.

"The other night we turned on the TV to see the
news, but the movie *Scream* was still on. I can hardly
describe it. There were three young people, completely psychopathic, with bloody knives, evoking

more and more terror. It's a rather sick forum in which to meet as Canadians."

I visited Janine Langan, the William J. Bennett professor of culture and Christianity at St. Michael's College at the University of Toronto, to find out why so much of popular culture and art seems designed merely to shock us.

We talked in the living room of her ivy-covered home, fifteen minutes from the university campus. Surrounding us were plants, a grand piano, books of paintings by Matisse, Gauguin and others.

Tucked away in a corner was a statue of Mary, a small reminder of Langan's deep Catholic convictions.

She compares the scene from *Scream* to the movies of the 1950s: they were dreamy, maybe even sentimental. The 1990s, and the decade's cultural products, are too often unacceptably sadistic.

She pulls out another example, an entry in this year's annual competition at London's prestigious Tate Gallery. Artist Tracey Emin came close to winning Britain's most-publicized art award by putting her bed on exhibit, complete with shrivelled condoms, a tampon, dirty panties, and sheets stained by semen.

"This is an excellent example that this culture has given up, accepting our worst urges as normal," she says.

Langan says Christianity is slowly losing its hold on the Western world's imagination. As the philosophical underpinnings of our society collapse, so do our manners – and our art.

She says an artist "should be delighted to be in the world, delighted to be surrounded by so much beauty, delighted to be himself a human in it and to be able to create like God himself."

For the past century, artists have been rejecting this notion, and the centuries-old partnership between art and the Catholic church has broken down.

Art sees itself as an alternative to that dead old thing – the church, she says. "It is a quest of freedom, a rejection of ideological art. I know what it rejects. I don't know what it embraces," she says.

"They have lost completely this sense that art shows up the heartbeat of the world, the fact that the world needs, that the world gives, and that we ourselves can respond to it, because both of us, the world and ourselves, are children of God, and are filled with this creative power that is in being itself."

Langan says she invites many of her students to modern art galleries. "They come out saying, 'I'm sure glad I'm not artsy,' but there is not one of them that doesn't think Van Gogh is a genius. He speaks precisely to that, that life is, that meaning is, that we have to extract the beauty out of it. This shock art doesn't do that at all."

* * *

She says we are in a downward cultural spiral because we have given up on the American Dream, and have found nothing to replace it. That dream is total freedom from the past, from God, from our own limitations, and from our responsibility to others.

One result is our society's increasing use of vulgar and blasphemous language.

"It is an expression of the total frustration of the population. You cannot strike at the cause of the problem, so you strike at God. It's about your last perception of the existence of God, that frustration.

"Vulgar language is a way of destroying your own image. It's part of this anti-hero culture in which we live, and in which anything that gives you the slightest hope of being anything great or beautiful or bigger than life is immediately torn down."

Shock art and vulgar language both have a common motivation she says: "If I will never be great, I will be as shameless as possible." Bad manners and vulgarity also have a common root: lack of gratitude for the gifts we receive from God and from others.

What Christianity and Judaism teach us is that "the world is amazing, a matter of immense creativity. It took six eras to build, and it is all aimed at making it possible for you to be the kind of person you are. It is an amazing gift."

The gratitude and delight that we feel in those rare moments of appreciation of Creation itself "is an unspontaneous experience of the sense of the presence of that which is greater. The other [vulgarity] is the spontaneous and conscious expression of the lack of that presence."

We are also indebted to others, but we are too busy worrying about what we want and need to notice others' contributions, says Langan. "Obviously, you cannot survive ten minutes without somebody doing something for you. So what it means is that you are closing your eyes to an avalanche of gifts."

We don't want to acknowledge that we are created beings, because it limits us and our freedom, she says.

"We don't want to be created, because there are all kinds of implications about that. Among other things, that you can't do anything you want, more simply that you don't own your own body. We can't do any old thing we want, literally, physically, however we might want to. You don't have to go to Christianity for this. All you have to do is read Aristotle or the Greeks."

What does this have to do with our relationship to God? I ask.

"God is that other, which is not me, and which I cannot control. There is very little sense today that that is a good thing. We do everything we can to ensure we don't get caught in a relationship with another that we can't control, certainly not with our parents, and certainly not with siblings, and certainly not with our girlfriend, and we hope to high heaven that if we get married, it doesn't mean we will get caught forever with this other that we cannot control.

"So there is this terror of being alone. That projects itself on God as well, or maybe it comes from our rejection of that original relationship."

The result? Joyless lives.

"What really makes it impossible to live joyously is being incapable of having any loving relationships with anybody, and that is enormously widespread."

Janine Langan was only thirteen when she first encountered the American Dream. She came from Paris to New York with her businessman father, and says, "I was totally astonished at this notion that 'forget yesterday, everything will be positive tomorrow.'" She says the American Dream is opposite to that of Europe, which sees tradition, including Christianity, as a bonus rather than a problem.

Her advice is to recapture some of that traditional wisdom and admit our own physical limits, our need for others, and our need for God. She says the world hates the Catholic church, and particularly Pope John Paul II, for pointing out such truths.

"Even though our church is drab in general, and a bit scared, and not very sophisticated, and not very well-educated, most of it, it is still a bastion holding up in its dusty way essential truths directly opposed to the choices its critics have made."

Why do so many intellectuals, such as poet T.S. Eliot, convert to Catholicism? I ask.

"The space that the church has carved in the mental world for people to meet God is so large, so superlative, so rich and so delighted with any creative input. That is not translated, certainly not in the media, and not even to our [Catholic] kids in the schools. Our kids know nothing about this tradition. Yet it is precisely what gives this space, the openness to so many lives, in so many ways."

Langan says the greatest phrase of all time is "Be still and know that I am God." Why? "Because it speaks of the most fundamental experience of being, which is that before you can speak, you have to stop the noise and hear. Once you are aware that you are created, then you can start physically manifesting this being: drawing, speaking, having ideas, making choices, but without that all the theories in the world are useless, because you will not understand them."

She believes in a consistent teaching of the Church fathers, that "outside the church there is no salvation." She says joining the church "gives you a vocation, a meaning for life. It gives you a leverage point on the whole society around you."

She compares joining the church to getting married. It is demanding, we don't understand what we're getting into when we join our lives, and it forces us to keep going when we wonder why we ever got into it. This commitment is essential if we are to persevere; ultimately it is also enriching.

She says our lives are meant to be what she calls a liturgy, a manifestation of the splendour of being, a way of making God tangible in the world. "That's a very important insight, that your life has to be a liturgy.

That's why it's not so great to blaspheme, why it's not so great to indulge in being ridiculous, laugh at yourself, and pour out the deepest dirt inside you in public, as though you enjoy eating your own vomit."

Liturgy is a word more familiar to Catholics than to me, so I ask what she means by a liturgy. A worship service, perhaps?

"I mean almost poem and show and concert, and everything that manages to do better than drab. A worship service which, at its best, in the church and in our lives, is a ritual that is reinvented every time, a poem, a symphony."

* * *

Langan received her first university degree at the age of eighteen, at Smith College, and went on to post-graduate degrees at the Sorbonne and the University of Indiana. But she and her husband, Tom Langan, a philosophy professor and president of Canada's Catholic Civil Rights League, have also found time for five children and nine grandchildren to date.

She is as comfortable with children as she is with Aristotle and Van Gogh. She looks a bit like a granny, cleans ovens and bakes cookies – but talks as tough as John Paul II.

She brings home the meaning of life as a liturgy in a down-home example. "When I think of liturgy, I always think of the birthday gifts kids give you. Your little children, they always make pictures. And you are ecstatic when you get these pictures. Anyone would say only a mother would love it, but the only reason a mother would love it is because she sees her love has not been spent for nothing. In that picture the best of this kid is being poured back to you. Maybe they only understand that much, but who cares, it's love."

Victoria Matthews

Anglican Bishop

Feminism has shattered Christianity's unthinking image of God as male, and reinterpreted its Bible, but has only begun to shake up an institution that has been ruled by men for most of 2000 years.

In Canada, there may be no better illustration of this cautiously post-feminist church than Victoria Matthews, Anglican bishop of Edmonton. She is no ardent feminist, but is one of only eleven women among 800 Anglican bishops around the world, and a contender to take over the reins of the Anglican Church of Canada when Archbishop Michael Peers retires as primate sometime in the early years of this new century.

Victoria Matthews was also the only female bishop appointed to the influential planning group for the 1998 Lambeth Conference, the meeting for bishops of the worldwide Anglican Church, held every ten years.

She is living proof of feminism's impact on the church, but says it is absurd to think of her as an expert on feminism.

"The humour of the situation is, I was elected by the church, then a group of men gathered around me, and laid on hands, and instantly I became an authority on women. In terms of symbolism, it's the church all over again. The men make the woman who's then going to be the spokesperson for the women."

It is a crisp, snow-covered November day as I drive up in a cab to the Anglican diocese office in south Edmonton. I am uncharacteristically early, and a tall blond woman in a beige trenchcoat is coming down the stairs with a large dog on a leash. The dog is Zeus, an eleven-year-old part-Rhodesian ridgeback; his constant companion is Canada's first female Anglican bishop.

Matthews surprises me by remembering, in detail, the ten-minute interview we had on the telephone in 1993, when she was first elected a suffragan, or assistant, bishop in Toronto. Subsequent interviews have blurred together, but, she says, that first avalanche of interviews as the world's fifth female Anglican bishop are burned into her mind.

Today, I want to know how feminism has changed the church, how it has changed Victoria Matthews, whether she thinks of God as a woman, and what's different about a female bishop. How much of her moderate feminism is due to political caution? I ask.

"The political caution, I have to say, is a reality, because as a bishop you can easily get yourself into too narrow a stream, and that limits your effectiveness. So I think you need to be able to speak across the breadth of the church. I would say that I have grown from being marginal to at least moderate now."

So what has feminism done for the church? She gives me a quick review. Feminist theologians have reminded Christians of all those biblical texts that illustrate the feminine relationship with the divine, like that in the New Testament (Matthew 23.37) where Jesus says he yearns to gather the people of Jerusalem together "as a hen gathers her chicks." And those other passages that suggest male contempt for women, such as the incident (Mark 14) in which Jesus says the woman who anointed him with perfume will be remembered wherever his good news is preached, yet the Gospel writer neglects to tell us her name.

There is also the feminists' attempt to present a fuller picture of the divine, through the notion of Sophia (Greek for wisdom), who is portrayed in Proverbs as a woman calling out to her people.

On a third level, the feminists have focused attention on what Matthews calls the "texts of terror," accounts of the rape and terrorization of women, and other biblical passages that have been used as excuses for domestic violence. "The history is abysmal and terrible," she says. "The more I read, the more I appreciate the fact that women have felt forbidden to own their relationship with God. It has always been seen as second-rate, and something that really comes through the divine."

Does the fact that Jesus was a man make it more difficult for women to relate to him, or to God?

"Certainly, some have experienced that. I have not. There's a wonderful joke: 'Why are all the pictures of Mary so sad? She was hoping for a girl.' Yes, there are those who say women cannot relate to a male saviour."

But she believes that Jesus was a revelation of the divine, and says that given the culture of 2000 years ago, "the incarnate one had to be male."

"Any revelation that is received comes through the lens of culture. You can't take a photograph from nowhere. So you always receive from where you are. It took us a long, long time to realize how culturally conditioned that revelation is."

But that cultural conditioning only goes so far. "We've allowed Jesus over the centuries to become blond and blue-eyed. We've no need to keep him Palestinian. We've not required that those who become priests in the church be born of a virgin, let alone Jewish. So it says more about our culture over the centuries that we get hung up about him being male."

The Roman Catholic Church denies ordination to women on the basis that women cannot represent Jesus in their persons. Opponents of women's ordination in the Anglican church, where women were first legitimately ordained in 1976, have a different emphasis: that there is no scriptural basis for women being priests.

Has Matthews ever had doubts about the legitimacy of her own ordination in 1980? "Certainly, before I was ordained, I thought a lot about it, and I have revisited it from time to time.... But all the way along, it has given me more concern about what it does to the ecumenical conversation. Out of courtesy you need to take it seriously as the Catholic and Eastern Orthodox churches voice their concerns."

Feminists say women necessarily bring a different perspective to Christianity than men do. What about Victoria Matthews? Does she bring a different perspective than a man to her preaching and to her relationships as bishop?

"I'm sure I have. Six years ago, when I was elected a bishop, I was reluctant to say that. But there's no doubt about it. I think that one of the things that brought it home was being at the Lambeth conference last year with about 800 Anglican bishops from around the world, and realizing that being one of the eleven women present was a unique opportunity, and a unique perspective."

Is she saying she didn't realize how much different her perspective was?

"Well, I knew it. Lambeth just highlighted it. I see the different perspective every week as I move around the diocese or around the country, that there have been patriarchal assumptions dominant, and they are being challenged. And the peculiar role that I have is that I'm in the role of a leader, which has been a patriarchal position, but that as a woman, I'm in a position to hear with a woman's ear."

I don't want to let her off the hook, so I ask how she is personally changing things.

"Well, it's difficult to say, because I can't say, 'When I was a man, I did such and such.' But one of the things I did, and a man could easily have done it, was choose to live in one of the neediest neighbourhoods of the city, and that has allowed me to do even more than I expected. When people get into those conversations that are inevitable, of denying poverty, and saying everybody's all right and nobody's hurting, I can say, 'Let me tell you where I live, and two doors down from me....' That's helpful."

Matthews' neighbourhood is home to drug dealers, prostitutes plying their trade, and the inevitable needles and condoms littering the streets. And there are condemned houses that have had to be torn down, because families with nowhere else to go insisted on moving in. Yet, she says, "it's a wonderful neighbourhood," and tells the story of how neighbours spotted a man coming out of her house while she was away, chased the thief and retrieved her portable computer.

How has feminism changed the church?

"We're preaching a kinder gospel in part, and I don't mean nicer. I mean kinder. I think that feminism speaks about women, but it has something to say to anyone with second-class status. We now have a more inclusive church. Thirty years ago, we built church after church where you had to go up a staircase to get in. And if you couldn't make the stairs, that was your problem. I'm moving this diocesan office for a couple of reasons, but one is that I will not have a non-accessible office. The first day I walked in, I knew I had to move.

"Feminism is the voice of the vulnerable, the voice that has known what it is to be despised. The voice that has known what it is to be abused. The voice that has spent more time observing than speaking, so that when it speaks, it speaks out of a wealth of observation, and usually with far greater awareness."

Matthews comes from a privileged background, and it shows in her confidence and social polish. As the daughter of a successful Toronto lawyer, she was sent to the private Bishop Strachan Anglican School. There, much to the surprise of her non-churchgoing family, she had an unexplainable religious experience one night that turned the teenager into a Christian, and ultimately into a bishop.

She chooses not to go into detail about her personal epiphany, but she offers this much: "I experienced for the first time the love of God. In my mind's ear, there also came a call to the priesthood."

Bishops and priests have traditionally been viewed as father figures. Do we need new images? I ask.

"I think we've got them. It just happens. One of the reasons, as a priest, that I didn't work very hard at pushing inclusive language for the godhead, and worry too much about inclusive language in hymns and so on, is because I was convinced, and still am, that when a woman stands at the altar, something louder than words is being heard."

Her actions also speak loudly on the issue of the continuing divisions within the Anglican Church on the ordination of women. She infuriated some of her fellow female bishops at the Lambeth conference by supporting a motion to continue tolerating opponents of women's ordination, who she says still number about 40 per cent of the world's 74 million Anglicans. In her own diocese, she appointed, to an Anglo-Catholic parish in Edmonton, a priest who questions the ordination of women.

Why did she do it? "I remember what it was like to be an ordained woman, or before that a laywoman, at a point when for many people it was unacceptable to favour the ordination of women. Now the power base is with those who believe in the ordination of women. The very thought that we would now legislate against people who are against the ordination of women is to legitimate intolerance. If it's the truth, and it obviously is, you don't need to protect it."

Will the Roman Catholic Church soon drop its opposition to the ordination of women?

"I go way out on a limb on this one. All the 'absolutely not' language in Rome tells me we're very close. Why is Rome talking about it in increasingly strong language? Because I think they see it coming. The Roman Catholic church has a pretty strong teaching of the voice of the faithful, and even though they've been told to be silent on the subject, the sense of the faithful is increasingly in favour of the ordination of women."

What does the ordination of women suggest about changes in our society? I ask. She delivers a zinger of an answer.

"That's a very disturbing question, not one I like. Does the ordination of women indicate a change in the hierarchical and patriarchal understanding of the church, and so it makes a significant difference? Or does the ordination of women simply prove that the church is no longer an institution of any importance in society? I'm not sure the answer is either, or it's something of both."

To Matthews, the greatest idea of all time is the possibility of a relationship with the divine, because it has the potential to bring us into wholeness and health and calls us into a fullness of being beyond anything we can imagine.

So, as our two-hour conversation winds down, I finally come to the question that ultimately proves to be the most interesting of all. What does a fully mature human being, in spiritual and emotional terms, look like? I suggest Mother Teresa as a feminine model. She suggests Jean Vanier, the Canadian-born founder of L'Arche homes for people with disabilities.

Jean Vanier is a gangling giant of a man, born to privilege as the son of governor general Georges Vanier. He became a Royal Navy officer, then a philosopher and an academic, before he began living with and caring for the severely handicapped. Mother Teresa was tiny, a child of poverty herself, and there was some doubt when she entered a convent that she had the stamina necessary for a teaching order.

Is Jean Vanier the male side of God, and Mother Teresa the female side? I ask.

"No, I wouldn't say that for a moment," she says. "Both are able to speak of incredibly simple things, and bring out of the simple things immense profundity that would seem almost a waste of time for someone else to say. Both have called the First World at least back to the concept of service, the concept of meaning, and a concept of selflessness. I don't think there is a male–female expression, a male face of the divine, a female face of the divine at all. Maybe what's fascinating about the two of them is that they're both paradoxical. She is the epitome of someone without power. Jean Vanier is the epitome of privilege and power who has chosen to be powerless, and to speak on behalf of the powerless. That is part of what makes them so arresting. But if Jean Vanier was female, and Mother Teresa was male, you would have two completely different people. I don't know whether I have just contradicted what I said earlier. Probably I did."

I press the debate. Jean Vanier may be in touch with his female side, as Matthews claims, but Mother Teresa at times was harshly critical and fiercely demanding. Does that make her more masculine? And what does that say about the nature of a God that Christianity has taught is neither male nor female, but has traditionally called "He" and depicted as male?

"If you were to describe the God you see in Jean Vanier and the God you see radiating in Mother Teresa, would that God be at all different? I don't think so. God is whole. God is above gender, beyond gender, inclusive of gender," she says.

God still sticks in my mind as being masculine. Christians describe the divine in masculine terms like king, judge and lawmaker, and I have trouble shaking that image from the ceiling of the Sistine Chapel: God as an old man with a white beard. How does Matthews see God?

"I don't want to get into this gender stuff, because that limits God profoundly, and does damage to God, but the whole notion of God wrapping her arms around an upset child is absolutely integral to my understanding of God. I realize the vocabulary of God's title is highly masculine, but the qualities are amazingly feminine.

"What is important is that God has personality. It's not an impersonal force, so there's the invitation to relationship. Certainly all these masculine titles have left a long legacy that have conditioned people, but the action and activity of God is highly feminine."

As I leave the interview, I can't help reflecting that maybe we're both right. God is neither male nor female, but we humans can't help seeing the divine in our own image.

The feminist revolution has just made it more possible for me to see Him as Her, and Victoria Matthews as a reflection of Her.

Ernie Regehr

Peace Activist

C hurches in Canada and around the world have permanently altered their attitudes to war, and Ernie Regehr of Waterloo has been one of the agents of change.

Since 1976, he has been part of Project Plough-shares, a peace research and lobby group supported by the Canadian Council of Churches. When Ernie Regehr started in the peace business, a Canadian diplomat told him to "go home and find something useful to do with your life."

"Today the environment has radically changed," says Regehr, the director of Project Ploughshares.

To find out why the churches have switched from justifying war to condemning it, and to explore what's needed to stamp out further war, I visited Canada's premier peace activist at his office in the basement of the Mennonites' Conrad Grebel College, at the University of Waterloo.

We talked with the window shades down, Regehr's laptop as a companion, and many chuckles at the absurdities of the real world and of a movie we both enjoy: *Dr. Strangelove,* the Peter Sellers satire of nuclear war.

As a Mennonite, he sees his role and that of Project Ploughshares as bearing witness in a centuries-old Mennonite way: showing an alternative to violence. But he has added to that Mennonite pacifist tradition a more activist form of witnessing: seeking out knowledge about the sources of conflict and acting to diminish that conflict.

* * *

Since at least the thirteenth century, when Thomas Aquinas articulated our modern version of the just-war theory, most of Christianity has maintained that war is justified under certain conditions, including as a just cause, as a last resort, and under a reasonable expectation that it will accomplish more good than evil.

But in the 1980s, churches in Canada and elsewhere began to struggle with the real threat of nuclear war. Their conclusion: "Under no circumstances can nuclear weapons be viewed as within the will of God."

"There is no ambiguity about nuclear weapons," says Regehr. "That is a cut and dried, black and white situation. No rational person can say that a weapon, the tiniest of which now is more destructive than the one that destroyed Hiroshima, is an instrument of security. To say we build them only so we don't have to use them is just a bit too much."

In 1982 and 1983, he and other church leaders met with prime minister Pierre Trudeau, and urged Canada to support a nuclear ban. The soul-searching that produced the churches' stand on nuclear arms led in turn to a reconsideration of the just-war theory.

By 1991, the majority of Canadian churches were condemning the Gulf War, and most would again oppose NATO action in Kosovo earlier this year; they were among the very few critical voices in both cases. It was a sea change in attitude, because Christian churches had separated themselves from the establishment and become a prophetic witness.

But Anglican bishops in England and American evangelicals supported the Gulf War. Why the differences among churches? I ask Regehr.

"It would be nice if theology drove politics," he says. "But I have the feeling that it is the other way round. We find theological rationales for the situation we are in. If the Canadian churches had not come through an active discussion in the 1980s of just-war ideas and whether or not nuclear weapons represented an acceptable form, it would have been very difficult for them to oppose the Gulf War in the 1990s. They would have been influenced by the public criteria: It was the invasion of another country, and a despot doing it," Regehr says.

He says the 1990s have seen more wars than any period since the Second World War. The difference is that now the wars are primarily civil wars, rather than wars between states. Project Ploughshares publishes an annual report on world conflicts, and recorded 36 armed conflicts in 1998, all of them civil wars. Most of them are poor countries in Africa, Asia or the Middle East.

So why are these poor countries at war? Because they lack resources, and try to take somebody else's?

"Most importantly, because they live in states that have not had the capacity to meet their fundamental needs. If you don't have the basic necessities of life, and you live in a region where the flow of small arms is all around you, it's not a surprise that you would try to avail yourself of this and try to change things. A Kalashnikov creates new options."

Most of today's wars are fought with firearms, and other small arms, such as landmines. This is why the Landmines Treaty signed in March 1999 in Ottawa was such a victory for peace, and why Regehr and other landmines activists are now mounting a campaign to control the sale of other small arms.

The devil's advocate in me asks: Why should we care about wars in other countries? "It's simply that we share a common humanity," he says. "You don't need much more reason than that. That's just the reality, and it is a reality. It's not an abstract idea. What affects people there affects people here. If we value life less there, then we're going to value life less here. If we take every measure we possibly can to insulate ourselves from the hurts of others, society is going to insulate itself from the hurts of my family. My aversion to the privatizing of medical care doesn't come out of a socialist ideology; it comes out of a fear of an ethic that says everybody should look after themselves, we don't look after each other."

Regehr says churches have generally come to believe that our safety depends on the security of all persons, a principle that has been dubbed the human security ethic.

"It is essentially the biblical premise that if you are worried about your own security, you inquire into the security of the other. So if you want to build up your own security, you should take measures that add to the security of your foe. None of these are new ideas. They were around at the time of Jesus and of Homer, but they became politically salient in the 1980s in response to the nuclear crisis."

I ask him to dream a little and imagine billions of dollars available to help poor countries pay off their debts and provide employment for their people, and bold new peace-making efforts to facilitate face-to-face talks in decades-old conflicts, such as the one in Cyprus. If all that were possible, how long would it take before there was no more conflict in the world?

His answer surprises me. "I don't think it would take that long. We're in a world where inter-state war is almost gone. That is quite a miracle. And it's not because there is no inter-state conflict. There is lots of it, more intense in many ways than it has been. But we've developed this astonishing array of trade regulations and so forth, and also a recognition that using military means to advance national interests is counter-productive.

"In many parts of the world, it is almost unthinkable that one state would go to war with a neighbouring state. And it is not just Europe. Uganda and Tanzania have historic differences, but they wouldn't go to war with each other. The Eritreans and the Ethiopians did.

"It is not nirvana yet, but inter-state war is a rare thing, and that is a product of design. The United Nations needs to be given some credit. It has built up mechanisms for dealing with conflict between states, but has had woefully inadequate mechanisms for dealing with conflicts within states. And that is what this human security ethic is starting to change now."

But he says we will probably never entirely eliminate war. The conflict in Kashmir between India and Pakistan is a political problem, and changes in economic or social conditions won't diminish the likelihood of war there.

Assuming that a few wars will always occur, what can we do about minimizing the damage?

"In the times when we are not at war, we should consciously think about and plan the way in which to conduct our conflicts. And if we are wise, we will divest ourselves of the most heinous forms of combat,"

Regehr says, referring in part to landmines and nuclear war.

He says there are mistakes aplenty, both in the ways we try to keep the peace, and in the ways we conduct war.

Canadian and other UN troops have been separating Greeks and Turks on the island of Cyprus for more than 30 years. "The people on each side have the notion that they understand each other perfectly, but they haven't spoken to each other in decades," he says. Canada and other countries are spending money on keeping peace, but what is really needed is some money and the will to bring people together in face-to-face talks.

Other mistakes: The West branded Slobodan Milosevic irrational, and then tried bombing, expecting an irrational person to make a rational decision in Kosovo, and starving Iraq by economic sanction, instead of building up and educating the civil society, the only real long-term hope of eliminating dictator Saddam Hussein.

Regehr says the best thing to do in Iraq is lift sanctions and send in non-governmental organizations to work with Iraqis. "Governments accountable to people are better than unaccountable governments. Democracies don't go to war with democracies, not because the leaders are innately more decent, but because they're accountable."

* * *

Another unanswerable question from Regehr: Why do we in the West spend so much money and time on Kosovo, or even Cyprus, where mere thousands have died, and almost entirely ignore the conflict in southern Sudan, where nearly two million have died?

Part of the answer, he says, is that the media tell us what's happening in Kosovo, but not in remote southern Sudan. One possible result is that there has been no serious international diplomatic attention to the problems of Sudan. Canada, for instance, has only one foreign service desk officer involved in Sudan, and he's responsible for Uganda, as well. That has begun to change only recently, when U.S. Secretary of State Madeleine Albright and Canadian Foreign Affairs Minister Lloyd Axworthy have shown new interest.

Canadians and other Westerners have also become obsessed with their own problems, he says. "Doug Roche [Canadian senator and anti-nuclear arms activist] once wrote in irony that in Canada the language of politics is the language of deprivation – taxes are too high, spending power too low. That's what animates Canadian politics. If you could just send half of the population to spend a couple of weeks in Bahr el Gazal [in southern Sudan], that would change the language."

I can't help but agree. My week-long stay in Bahr el Gazal earlier this year certainly taught me a new appreciation of the havoc wrought by poverty, and its sisters, war and despair.

Regehr says he has many moments of doubt about the usefulness of his work. But he's feeling optimistic at the moment. Among the hopeful signs he sees are: A decline in the number of wars over the 1990s, the landmines treaty, the new small-arms campaign, and pressure from heads of state in Ireland and Sweden and from Lloyd Axworthy for prohibition of nuclear weapons.

"It's a huge change in political consciousness. These are voices that are not just marginal Ploughshares peaceniks. I'm optimistic on these grounds, but then you go into Sudan, or the slums of Kingston, Jamaica: places of extraordinary despair. How do you put those two things together?" he asks.

What is the greatest idea of all time? I ask. Ernie Regehr is an activist, not a theologian, so he groans – or maybe it's a prayer.

"Oh, God! Well, the children's story in church on Sunday was a nice little analogy. We had this big gallon of maple sap. If you boil it all down, you get this little container of maple syrup, and if you boil that all down, what you get is this tiny maple candy. Then if you look at the Bible the same way, you can boil it all down to this: Love God and love your neighbour as yourself."

If we truly loved our neighbour, would we still have war? I ask.

"Presumably not," he says. "I have no idea what the greatest idea is, but I know that human security is better than nuclear deterrence."

Ron Sider

Co-founder of Evangelicals for Social Action

R on Sider doesn't want much: only one per cent of the salaries of the world's Christians. And it's for a good cause – the world's poorest people.

But his math is astounding. Christians have a total annual income of $10 trillion, and if they gave just $1 out of every $100, they could improve the living standards of the world's poorest billion people by 50 per cent in just one year.

And then Sider piles on fact after fact. Thirty-four thousand children die every day of hunger and preventable disease. Seventeen million people die every year from infectious and parasitic diseases we know how to prevent.

The message is clear, and Sider spells it out. "It is objectively immoral when you've got massive poverty, and very wealthy Christians who are ignoring it. That's a sin."

What's surprising is that his message is so popular.

Twenty-two years ago, this little-known Canadian theology professor at Eastern Baptist Theological Seminary near Philadelphia amassed the facts and figures on poverty, and did the math on what it would cost his fellow Christians to make a difference. The result was one of the best-selling evangelical Protestant books of the century: *Rich Christians in An Age of Hunger.*

The book has now sold close to 400,000 copies, and keeps on selling. It also helped create America's fast-growing movement of eight to ten million socially conscious evangelicals, with Ron Sider as one of its best-known leaders. He is a co-founder of Evangelicals for Social Action, and founder of Creation Care, a Christian ecological journal.

* * *

As I take a cab to his home in Philadelphia, I realize I am entering another world. It's not only an inner-city neighbourhood of boarded-up storefronts, but also an America of born-again presidential candidates, and a fervent evangelicalism unequalled for its political clout. It is far removed from the Mennonite farm where Ron Sider grew up on the Canadian side of the Niagara River.

He lives the simple lifestyle he preaches. He and his wife, Arbutus, a family therapist, give 30 per cent of their incomes to the poor. In the 1970s, they bought their home in a racially mixed neighbourhood for $15,000, and they still buy many of their clothes in the neighbourhood thrift shop. He says his best suit, a pinstripe that he wears in his Washington political appearances, cost him just $25.

In person, he's relaxed and anything but a guilt-monger. His two-storey home is simple and boasts a woodstove in the kitchen, but it is as comfortable and spacious as much more expensive suburban homes.

"I really don't want people to be overwhelmed with guilt," he says. "I was speaking at a Bible College, and a very sincere missionary wife on furlough at home in America stood up and said she felt guilty using fluffy towels after seeing the poverty in the Third World. I told her to enjoy the fluffy towel. This world is full of splendour. I want everybody to enjoy the good things."

Sider says he himself is not living out the full implications of his book. All he asks of Christians is that they consider what more they could do to help others, and begin to take the smallest steps forward.

He stumbled into what has become his true vocation of popularizing complex subjects. While simultaneously completing a theology degree and a Ph.D in history at Yale, he gave a sermon at a small Baptist church about a principle that has become a foundation of his later writings. He calls it the graduated tithe: giving away 10 per cent of the household income needed for a no-luxuries basic lifestyle, and 15 per cent of every $1,000 above that. The sermon became a lifestyle, then a magazine article, and eventually the book which will always be better remembered than the dozen or so he has written since.

When Sider wrote *Rich Christians in an Age of Hunger,* he knew almost nothing of economics, had never taken an ethics course, and had spent just a few weeks in the Third World. How did he know what to write?

"If you read the Bible, there are hundreds of verses about the poor and justice," he says.

The book has been revised and updated since that original 1977 edition. Its economics are more sophisticated, and the 20th anniversary edition is now a fact-filled shortcut to an understanding of global economics, Third World poverty, and what ordinary people can do about it. It is also a passionate biblical argument that true Christian commitment will change the world.

Sider's suggestions include not only micro-loans so the Third World poor can develop their own businesses, but also partnering suburban and urban churches to revitalize inner-city ghettoes in the U.S., and political lobbying like the church world's Jubilee 2000 campaign to pay off the debts of the world's poorest countries.

What is your hope for the poor 50 years from now? I ask.

"I wouldn't need 50 years. I would need 20. Poverty is awful, it warps and distorts people. God doesn't want that; God wants wholeness for every person. And God calls people to be especially engaged in that. If we had even one out of the eight people claiming to be Christian really committed to doing what needs to be done, we would dramatically reduce poverty."

He believes Christianity can produce both a spiritual and material transformation. It helps people kick drugs and alcohol, straightens out marriages, and reduces poverty. World views make a difference, he says, and cites Hinduism's untouchables and India's poverty as an example. "A world view that says you are down at the bottom because you made bad choices in your previous incarnation doesn't encourage any significant change," says Sider.

"Of course there are people who are living with integrity and spreading joy, who are secularists and Buddhists, etc. I respect that, but I'm quite ready to argue that historic Christian theism is the best way to go. It's also true, and it leads to great happiness."

* * *

In his latest book, *Just Generosity,* Sider argues that it would be possible to scientifically prove his point, by comparing secular social programs with faith-based programs. One of the examples he cites as evidence of the difference faith makes is Lawndale Community Church in Chicago. Twenty years ago, the neighbourhood was one of the 20 poorest in the U.S., with infant mortality levels at near-Third World levels. With the help of suburban churches, the Chicago Bears football team and others, Lawndale Community Church has since been able to turn that around. Its social ministries have grown into a $10 million a year program, 22 doctors are working at one-third salary in its clinic, and the infant mortality rate has dropped by 60 per cent.

The Lawndale church has also coupled all that with quiet person-to-person evangelism. Sider says "literally hundreds and hundreds of very broken, very dysfunctional people have come to personal faith, and their lives have been transformed. They got married for the first time, or they got their marriages back together, and many of them have become good parents.

"People today have to choose between a radically individualistic post-modern relativism, where each person creates their own meaning, value and truth, and historic Christianity, where truth is objective and where God has told us what is right and wrong," he says.

He is as conservative in his reliance on the Bible, and what it has to say about the family and sexuality, as he is liberal on social justice issues.

Sider says the postmodern marriage operates on the principle that "I need to be true to myself," and when problems inevitably arise in a marriage, he says that view will lead to divorce and to fatherless children who are statistically more prone to troubles with the law, teenage pregnancy, drug abuse, and problems in forming their own intimate relationship.

"I regularly say it's just as difficult to follow Jesus today in the area of sex and family as it is in the area of money and care for others," he says.

"Christian marriage means an egalitarian relationship between husband and wife, it means exclusive sexual commitment. Unfortunately many Christian marriages break up, too, but if you can live that out in all its goodness in the midst of the hell of today's agony in the family, that is powerfully attractive."

What is the greatest idea of all time? I ask.

"That the creator of 120 billion galaxies loves us so much that he became flesh and died for us," he says.

Do you ever have any doubts? I ask. "I think any thinking person in the modern world does. But I'm a historian and I looked pretty carefully at the evidence about Jesus' life and resurrection. There are really sound grounds for thinking Jesus was alive on the third day. And the second thing is that Christianity works. The only thing that really blocks me is the church. If the gospel is the good news of the kingdom, then people in this new order should live differently. But so much of the church is so conformed to culture, it isn't really obvious it's a radical new community."

I try to cut to the point: "What you are saying is that so much of the church is not living out the gospel that you wonder if it's true."

"Yeah," says Sider.

His books are directed at the 45 per cent of Americans who go to church every Sunday, because he believes that is his best hope of recruiting the numbers that will make a difference to a suffering world.

"My biggest concern now is that we won't have enough Christians who care. And it won't happen without a religious revival. So the biggest part of my time now is with movements praying for revival," he says.

John Stackhouse

Former President of the Canadian Evangelical Theological Association

John Stackhouse is one of the very few evangelical Protestants in Canada who thinks God should be dropped from the Constitution.

The supremacy of God was inserted into the preamble to the Charter of Rights and Freedoms in 1982, primarily as a result of pressure from evangelicals, and John Stackhouse happens to be a former president of the Canadian Evangelical Theological Association. But on this issue, he has more in common with MP Svend Robinson and the Canadian Humanist Association, who say it's discrimination to invoke God in the Constitution of a nation with a rising number of non-believers.

"We do not insist on monotheistic belief as a condition for citizenship in Canada," Stackhouse says. "Since we don't insist on that, we shouldn't have belief in God, even implicitly, involved with the documents that frame our common life."

I wanted to know how Christianity can find its place in a multicultural Canada, and John Stackhouse obviously had something to say on the subject, so I travelled to Vancouver to see him.

He taught modern Christian history at the University of Manitoba until a year ago, and is now the Sangwoo Youtong Chee professor of theology at Regent College, an influential evangelical institute of Christian studies affiliated with the University of British Columbia. We talked in his tiny office, a space cluttered with books, computer, and the guitar and bass he plays at the college and his Anglican church. Also decorating his office were some hand-drawn pictures of bugs and butterflies, courtesy of six-year-old Devon, the youngest of his three sons.

Didn't we start out as a Christian country? I ask.

"Europeans came to Canada partly to discover stuff, partly to grab stuff, but in many cases they came to make this an outpost of missionary work, which isn't the same as the American founding, where they came to escape repressive regimes in Europe. So the Canadian story is a more missionary story," he says.

He traces today's Canadian civic values back to Christianity. He says constitutional government, science and human rights all arose out of Christian roots. "No culture has gone after slavery the way Christian culture has. No culture has empowered women the way Christian culture has."

Yet, he says, Confederation was a business deal, a practical arrangement. "That has been the essential genius of Canadian political life, that we will opt in if it is in our interest to do so, and if it no longer looks like a good deal, we will think of backing out again. That explains an awful lot of Canadian political history.

"What I'm suggesting is that Canada wasn't a sacred project. Quebec had a sense of sacredness, of being a French Catholic bastion. But the project itself isn't couched in sacred language."

Christianity is in a unique position in Canada because it was dominant when the country was formed, and dominant until about the 1960s, when many people started to quit taking it seriously. So what do we as a nation do about Christianity as we enter the 21st century?

One thing we should *not* do, says Stackhouse, is eliminate religion altogether from our common life.

"There has been a kind of implicit prejudice, an orthodoxy that has been imposed on public speech, that says you have to prune your language of every reference to the supernatural. You have to couch your speech in terms of reason and experience and whatever happens to be the faddish philosophy of the moment, and that's the only way you're going to be heard on CBC or in the *Globe and Mail*. I think that's anti-democratic, and it's anti-liberal in the strong sense of the term.

"People should be free to invoke any truth they like, and if a majority of voters find it powerfully convincing for someone to recite from the Koran, or read from the Christian Bible, or quote from Karl Marx, people should be free to do that. That would be an honest pluralism."

One exception to such verbal freedom would be teachers in our public schools. They are hired to teach subjects such as mathematics and science, and to model shared Canadian values, including neighbourliness and pluralism. They are not hired to teach their own religion, he says.

"But all of us are located in a particular outlook. We can't escape that; none of us can be completely objective. I would not have any trouble with a teacher saying 'I'm a Jew' or 'I'm a Muslim' and then trying to model to the students how one can be a citizen, how one can discipline that outlook in the educational situation."

Stackhouse says anti-Christianity sometimes shows up in Canadian public life, particularly among those journalists or officials who come from the baby boom generation, and are still rebelling against the repressive religion of their parents.

Now that Christianity is no longer dominant, however, the next generation will likely be just un-Christian, not anti-Christian, he says. Christianity will then be able to make its way with every other alternative.

Why should we take religion seriously in schools and public life? He responds with three good reasons:

"You simply can't explain the human individual and human societies without talking about religion.

You can't understand the history of Canada without understanding the missionary impulse. You can't understand political life, art, or even economics.

"Why did Adam Smith write *On the Wealth of Nations*? He was trying to bring another point of view on what he saw as an immoral economic situation in the eighteenth century, and was hoping this would be more just and fair and kind. According to what? According to Christian principles."

Secularization has also failed to kill religion, he says. As the 20th century ended, it was making a comeback.

And, finally, "Religion is scarier than it was 50 years ago in Canada, when two out of three Canadians went to church every Sunday, and our immigration policy was such that you probably wouldn't get into Canada if you weren't a Christian. Religion is a more divisive force now than it has ever been in Canadian life, because we have more religions, and new religions. People actually know what a Sikh is now."

My experience is that Canadians are more willing to talk about religion than they were even ten years ago. I ask him what he thinks.

"That's definitely true. People are more willing. And they're especially willing to talk about religion if we call it spirituality instead. In that semantic preference of spirituality, we're seeing this reaction against the cultural dominance of Christianity. So when people say, 'I'm not religious, I'm spiritual,' what they mean is, 'I'm not a member of a religious faith, and I'm certainly not going to take my orders from the authorities in religion.' It's a turn towards the individual self as the arbitrator of what is good and bad. I think this is pretty profound."

If religion is more divisive than ever, then how are we going to survive together?

Stackhouse says one thing we need to do is get past the idea that in religion it is somehow immoral to think your view is superior to another's. We all cheerfully endorse different ideas about economics or politics or hockey teams, and even enjoy debating the differences. So why can't we do the same in religion?

"Christians think our religion is better than others, because we offer Jesus, but we can still appreciate that there is goodness and truth and beauty in other religions. There is nothing unique or Christian about that. Muslims feel that, Buddhists feel the same way. Hindus feel the same way."

What would happen if we just backed off and said all other points of view are equally valid?

"That's an ideal that has never been achieved. No one thinks that all views are equally good. No one thinks that National Socialism is just as good as the Judaism it tried to exterminate. We all think that some religions are better than others, some values are better than others."

He believes Canada is in a good position to model a new kind of pluralism for the world. He says we may be the first nation to face the problem of maintaining a common life without reference to transcendent values or other common resources that can help us deal with divisive questions, such as abortion or homosexuality.

"The American experiment, which arguably was the first country to try to have a common life without requiring any particular religious conformity, at least has a common ideology, as to what is and isn't un-American. In Canada, we have even less.

"We have all these various religious and philosophical outlooks that are bound together by a common economy, and not much else. We don't have any kind of heroic history to come back to, we don't have a strong sense of ethnicity, we don't have heroes the way our European neighbours do."

Stackhouse says Canada and other nations are already developing what he calls a "true-blue pluralism" that will make decisions not on the basis of any tradition, but on the basis of a democratic vote.

So, if this true-blue pluralism comes to pass, how is Christianity going to cope? It hasn't had much experience at living side by side with other religions. It is a missionary religion, charged with the responsibility to convert the non-believer.

He begs to differ. He says Christianity can and does offer what it thinks to be a superior message, without seeking to impose it politically on anyone else.

He says Christianity is in a unique position in Canada, because it used to dominate the culture, and now non-Christians are watching as it learns to deal with its loss of influence. If Canadian Christians could learn to get along with fellow Christians and fellow Canadians, they could set an example of pluralism not only for other Canadians, but also for the world, he says.

But first they have to move away from the stereotypes they're locked in. "A kind of capitulation to contemporary liberal culture where we don't want to impose our views on anybody else, and we don't even want to have anything distinctive to say. Or the conservative stereotype, trying to roll the clock back to a golden age of Christian Canada, where we get to have our songs sung in public schools, where we get to have our prayers said in public ceremonies, and we get to have our morals, and only our morals, manifested in the law books."

As our conversation winds down, I remember the question I've asked all the religious thinkers I have interviewed: What is the single greatest idea of all time?

"That God was in Christ reconciling the world to himself," says Stackhouse.

It is a predictable answer for an evangelical, so I ask why he thinks it's the greatest idea. "If it's true that the one true God took human form in Jesus of Nazareth, then we not only have prophets and mystics, and other spiritual adepts who can gesture toward the divine. We actually have God there to look at."

But John Stackhouse has an ace up his sleeve. "And if we suppose that God was not in Christ, I would still argue that it may be the greatest idea. If one looks at the historic impact of Christianity, an impact that's only growing in the 20th century, and into the 21st, if God is not in Christ reconciling the world to himself, then Christianity is a misbegotten faith. The world's most successful religion is a mistake, and all the benefits have been happy accidents, and as quickly as possible, people need to be apprised of their foolish condition."

I ask if he ever has any doubts that Jesus is the revelation of God.

"Yeah, I do. The authority of the Bible is a difficult question to sort through at a scholarly level, given the 200-plus years of scholarly storm clouds surrounding it, when virtually everything in the Bible is disputed by some well-credentialed scholar."

But the problem that causes him the most doubts is that of evil, and it is one he examined in his book *Can God Be Trusted? Faith and the Challenge of Evil.*

"The idea that God is all good and all powerful is really a hard position to defend in the light of nature and the newspaper, so much so that if I weren't a Christian, I would be an atheist."

Stackhouse says that for him, Jesus' life and death are powerful reasons to believe that God is all he says he is, and he can imagine him at work in Kosovo or Rwanda.

"If Jesus is just a prophet who says God's good, well, I'd say he isn't. But if Jesus is God, and I can see Jesus being compassionate, that's the comforting side, the confirming side of the Christian belief that God is in Christ."

John Stackhouse's argument amounts to a polite rejection of other forms of monotheism. He couldn't be a Jew, or a Muslim, because a prophet's word is not enough to convince him that God is good, when the world often seems so obviously evil.

It's not an argument calculated to win him friends outside of Christian circles. But it is a demonstration of what he calls true-blue pluralism. Speak your piece boldly, and let the audience decide whether to agree.

Will Sweet

Philosopher

Technology has always challenged religion, says philosopher Will Sweet. "The difficulty now is that everything is being challenged. Giving up your faith isn't the answer. If you're a person of faith, you have to respond intelligently."

The invention of the printing press in the fifteenth century helped launch Protestantism and break the Roman Catholic Church's hold on Western Europe. In the seventeenth century, Galileo proved the earth revolves around the sun and the Inquisition sentenced him to house arrest. In the nineteenth and 20th centuries, archeology and carbon dating shattered some believers' idea that the earth was created between 6000 and 10,000 years ago.

At the dawn of the 21st century, says Will Sweet, technology's challenges to faith come at us from every direction: the Internet serves up pornography, the media spread other religions, and cryogenics offers the possibility of a kind of eternal life.

On the wall of his office at St. Francis Xavier University in Antigonish, Nova Scotia, are framed copies of some of his eleven earned degrees, including three doctorates. He grew up in Ottawa, so two of those three doctorates are from Ottawa's Carleton and Saint Paul Universities; the other is from the Sorbonne in Paris.

* * *

"Technology is not value-neutral, because the people who develop technology have values," says Sweet. "The technological world view sees nature as purely an instrument to be used to satisfy human wishes, and sees human reason as way of harnessing the environment. It doesn't think that whatever religions represent is real."

He says there are thinkers like Jacques Ellul who see technology as a sign of Man's fall from grace, and believe that paradise was a paradise without technology. "That's not my view at all. The things that humans create are signs of our own creativeness, but we shouldn't let ourselves think that we're the ones in charge."

Will Sweet is a churchgoing Catholic, and his long list of publications includes many on metaphysics, post-modern religion, and God as an object of philosophical argument, as well as technology and religious belief.

In the West, where technology is especially visible, it is oriented to the individual, and one of the results is a breakdown of community and social structures, he says. "Technology is a great leveller. The idea of hierarchy, the idea of authority just doesn't have the same sort of purchase anymore. Authority now has in some cases to be earned, because technology can always challenge whoever is in authority. Bill Gates is now the wealthiest man in the world, but somebody could come along five years from now and become the wealthiest person."

Technology reinforces whatever trends there are in culture, simply by spreading new ideas faster and more widely than ever before.

Among the trends reinforced by technology: individualism, optional religious commitment, and the notion of choice in religion. "It can be communicated by travel, or by television, where you can easily see a dozen different cultures in any week."

In the eighteenth century, philosopher Immanuel Kant said, "Two things fill the mind with ever-increasing admiration and awe: The starry heavens above and the moral law within."

"You can see that," says Sweet, "because you can imagine at the end of the eighteenth century you look up at the sky and see the magnificence of the heavens, and imagine something greater than you are, and it's regular and orderly. But now we live in cities, and you can't see the stars at night. The opportunity to encounter the transcendent is removed from us.

Nature is always mediated through television or computers. It is not encountered directly."

He says many of his students have a similar lack of understanding of what Kant had to say about the moral law within.

The starry heavens are supposed to remind us that there is something greater outside us and that we don't set all the rules. But today, we have so many choices, and if technology is our god, then we will buy into any new trend that comes across the Internet. We have a radical awareness of our own autonomy.

"The technological age says there are options. If you have sex with this woman, you don't have to have a child. You don't have to stay with this wife. You can think of sexuality as something you do for fun, and it's separated from the context in which sexuality used to take place. It has become a shopping mall kind of thing."

Technology has also contributed to the breakdown of community, he says. We can order up our own choice of television program almost at will, or microwave our own dinner. We can work alone, eat alone, recreate alone and participate in a religious service vicariously on television.

Because community has broken down, in the workplace, in religion, in universities, and even in the family, we get few challenges to our actions. "The computer doesn't say what I am doing is wrong, or a mistake."

Without a family or a church or close friends with a strong moral point of view, we are unlikely to find anyone to tell us what we are doing is odd or peculiar or even wrong, he says.

He says our innate consciences are still alive, however.

"We've been told that morality is ultimately a matter of personal preference/conscience, subjective choice. People get confused. I talk to students and ask them is there anything absolutely wrong? Some will say, 'Maybe torturing babies.' And I say, 'Let's not play philosophy class. Do you really believe it's right to torture babies?' And, no, there's still a moral sense. But you have to call people to it."

Even in the churches, many leaders are questioning the truth of the biblical text, and their own tradition's teaching. "If you can't go back to the text, because it is sort of vanishing, and you can't go back to the tradition, because it isn't there, where do you go back to?" he says.

"I think this interest in the New Age is because they're looking for something and can't find it in the old sources. If I turn on my computer, I can find thousands of places that provide spiritual enlightenment. We've lost all these anchors. Therefore religious belief has changed. If I lose that tradition, that text base, then spirituality is whatever I feel."

Sweet says many people see organized religion as an opponent of individual spirituality, but "I don't think you can have a real sense of spirituality unless you have some sense of community, of tradition."

How should religion deal with technology and the radical individualism it promotes? I ask.

"Aristotle says a good man doesn't take pleasure in evil things. So in a technological world, if you are a person at sea, then technology is not going to provide any breaks at all. If you are a person of faith it provides a challenge. Religion has to teach people to deal with technology, and by and large it doesn't."

He says we still pay attention to experts in economics or science, but we need to start paying attention to moral and religious experts. "When I'm confronted with an information glut, I need someone to say that's a waste of time, and that's important. And I can see the church playing a role in that."

He says *Humanae Vitae*, the 1968 encyclical from Pope Paul VI that prohibited Catholics from using artificial means of birth control, predicted that if we have this technology we will use it, and it will have social consequences. The prediction was accurate, he says: "It has increased the commodification of individuals; we treat people as objects and means to our own ends, and it encourages people not to make commitments. The technology becomes seductive, and once you have it, there are no brakes on it. If I develop this fixation with pornography, what's to stop me? My conscience? Hierarchy provides brakes, and sometimes it tells you to do things that you don't want to do, but that's probably a good thing. The church needs to play that role, or else we will just pursue our desires."

I object. How can the Canadian or American bishops, or John Paul II, keep track of, much less react to, the enormous volume of media, or the wave after wave of developments in bioethics and a thousand other fields?

"If you're an isolated individual and you're waiting for Rome to give you a call and say don't watch such-and-such a TV show, then it's not going to happen. But if you're a part of a community of people and realize that religion is not just a small part of your life, then you've got the tools to resist."

Sweet says to help their members deal with the changes brought by technology, churches will have to encourage more community among their members, and help the clergy to be more prayerful, more informed and more visible in the schools and other parts of the community.

"Religion can't be lived in a solitary way," he says. "Religion is going to be the last vestige of real community people have open to them, not just with the people around them who are spiritually united, but with a history.

"It provides us with a structure in which faith can be concretely lived. It provides a very real, tangible connection between myself and the divine."

* * *

What is the greatest idea of all time? I ask.

The self, says Will Sweet. It is a relatively recent concept that began to be articulated around the time of Christ, and became clearer in the sixteenth century. Until then, people saw themselves as part of a community, and had little concept of their separation from the environment, or perception of choice in life options.

He says technology has changed our perception of the self, by providing more and more ways to distinguish ourselves from others: more career possibilities, more options in family life, and more choices in sexuality and religious belief. Everything becomes optional, and the self becomes entirely distinct from its surroundings.

"This is the frightening thing now. People have so many options, they are at sea, they have lost track of what connects them to other people. We are hyper-aware of our being selves now. That probably explains the sense of anomie people in the West seem to be experiencing.

"Unfortunately, it challenges our human relations, and our access to something other than the purely natural disappears," he says.

"If we don't see God in other people, if we don't see God in nature, what does God become?"